This book of prayers is dedicated
to Harold Gieseke
who, when I was younger,
taught me the ministry of prayer

# Tough Days and Talks with God

This book presented

to

**Matt Gruntman**

*in honor*

of

**Confirmation**

4386-69, BROADMAN SUPPLIES. NASHVILLE, TENN.

# Tough Days and Talks with God

## Dean Nadasdy

**AUGSBURG** Publishing House • Minneapolis

**TOUGH DAYS AND TALKS WITH GOD**
Prayers for Young Teen Boys

Copyright © 1989 Augsburg Publishing House

Scripture quotations unless otherwise noted are from the Holy Bible: New International Version. Copyright 1978 by the New York International Bible Society. Used by permission of Zondervan Bible Publishers.

Photos: Dave Anderson, 16, 48; Jeffrey High, 36; Skjold Photographs, 66; Rohn Engh, 90; Joanne Meldrum, 102.

---

### Library of Congress Cataloging-in-Publication Data

Nadasdy, Dean, 1947–
    Tough days and talks with God : prayers for young teen boys / Dean Nadasdy.
      p.    cm.
    Summary: A collection of prayers for teenaged boys focusing on personal concerns, family members, friends, important events, holidays and celebrations, Biblical characters, and the future.
    ISBN 0-8066-2399-3
    1. Teenage boys—Prayer-books and devotions—English.  [1. Prayer books and devotions.]  I. Title.
BV4855.N33 1989
242'.832—dc19                               89-429
                                            CIP
                                            AC

---

Manufactured in the U.S.A.              APH 10-6680

2   3   4   5   6   7   8   9   0   1   2   3   4   5   6   7   8   9

# Contents

But deliver us from evil    99
For thine is the kingdom, and the power,    100
   and the glory, forever and ever. Amen.

## Questions about the Future    101

# About This Book

Some of these prayers were written on an airplane. That doesn't mean they're any better than prayers written on earth, which may seem a little farther from heaven. As I was writing them on an airplane, though, a woman sitting next to me asked what I was working on. She was friendly and, she said, a Christian, too. I told her that I was working on a prayer book for teen boys. She smiled and said, "Now there's an oxymoron if I've ever heard one."

An oxymoron is a phrase with two terms in it that just don't fit. "Jumbo shrimp" is an example of an oxymoron. How can something be a shrimp and jumbo at the same time? My friend on the airplane said, in her opinion, prayer books and teen boys just don't go together. It would be like putting air conditioners and Eskimos together. That is what she felt—that teen boys and prayer books are a bad match.

I'm not sure how you ended up with this book in your hands. It could have come to you as a gift, and maybe you secretly wish you would have received something else. Growing up, I had an aunt who liked to give me books like this one. To be honest, I didn't look much at a lot of them, but one book of prayers became very important to me. For me, I think it had a lot to do with learning how to pray.

The prayers in this book allow you to learn to pray real prayers—prayers that reflect life as you live it. Prayer books are not meant to replace prayers that you speak in your own words. They can help, though, when you're trying to put into words for your Lord what you feel inside.

In many ways, our prayers with God are learning events. For example:

▶ In prayer, we can discover what God's will is for our lives;

▶ In prayer, we learn that we depend on God and that we can't make it through life alone;

▶ In prayer, we learn how much we jlove God and how much God loves us. We learn how important it is to keep talking with God if our relationship is to remain strong; and

▶ In prayer, we learn how to care for others and serve them as we pray for their needs.

I hope the prayers in this book teach you all of that and more. I hope these prayers teach you that anything on your mind and in your heart is OK to bring to God in prayer. Your prayers don't have to be in special "church" language, either. God wants to hear from you in words that are real about things that are real. That's why these prayers are in language like yours and are about everything from Corvettes to hot lunch cooks.

There are eight categories of prayers. "About My Room . . . about My Life" is a section of prayers that are pretty personal. These are prayers just between you and your Lord about important things in your life. "Friendship Prayers" are prayers for and about your friends. "Family Prayers" give you a chance to pray for the people in your family (even a brother or sister if you have one). "Before and After Prayers" can be spoken at the start and at the end of important events. "Prayers for Big Days" are holiday and celebration prayers. "Prayers about People in the Bible and Me" give you a chance to open your Bible and find yourself having a lot in common with 11 people in the Bible. "Prayers on the Lord's Prayer" help you understand the different parts of the prayer Jesus gave us to pray. Finally, "Questions about the Future" are prayers that may never be answered until the year 2020 or later, but it helps to pray about the future. Prayers for the future give us confidence and hope.

So there you have it. I wish I could meet that woman on the airplane again. She was convinced that teen boys never would use a prayer book. I disagree, and I'd tell her so. I have evidence, too. What evidence? Why, you, of course, with a prayer book in your hands and a prayer, just now, coming to your lips.

# ► About My Room . . . ◄
## about My Life

# ▶ About my room . . . about my life

One thing that really bugs me, Lord,
is the way I get hassled about my room.
So it's messy. So it's really *messy*.
So some creeping thing might appear pretty soon
if I don't clean under the bed.
So my socks might get up and walk on their own.
It's my room, Lord! It's my space!

I like my room, Lord.
It may not always (or hardly ever) look good.
It may not even smell good, but it's mine.
Maybe that's why I get so upset when people
criticize my room, or call it a warehouse,
or say it smells like a locker room.

My room is me, Lord.
That's what people don't understand.
Do you understand, Lord? Do you?
Maybe my room is sort of like my life—
I don't have everything lined up and in order yet.
I am still trying to decide what goes where,
and what's important,
and what I should keep and what I should throw out.

I know. I do need help. It is a mess.
If it's true that "cleanliness is next to godliness,"
you and I could get a little closer.
I'll work at it, Lord. Honest. Even I worry about
those sounds I hear from under my bed. Amen.

Lord, I love to be popular!
I like it when people like me.
I can tell, too, when I'm a hit or a bomb.
People's faces show it.
Their eyes light up. They smile. They cheer me on.
Or they look at me
as if I were someone fresh off a ship from Mars.
I hate that look.

"What's hot and what's not,"
is the title of many magazine articles.
You know me well enough, Lord,
to know I want to be considered hot.

I know this can be dangerous, Lord.
I know that wanting everyone to like me
can make me do some pretty bad things
just to be liked.

In Romans 12:1-2 you warn against
being "conformed to the world."
You want me to see
that being popular with people
is not as important
as being in tune with you and your will for my life.

So, Lord, whether I'm hot or not,
keep me committed to doing what pleases you. Amen.

Lord, I'm here to praise you for unsung heroes.
I'm grateful for the 20-game winners
and the latest rock star
and the newest addition to the hall of fame.
Right now, though, I'd like to thank you
for the heroes who never get trophies
but who definitely deserve to be called heroes.

Thank you, Lord,
for my parents who are always there for me;
for the teacher who keeps teaching well
even though no one says thanks;
for the paramedics who save people's lives every day;
and for the coach who keeps us working on lay-ups
until we get it right.

Thank you for police officers and firefighters
who are just 911 away;
for nurses sitting at hospital bedsides late at night;
for pastors who work 60 hours a week
when everyone thinks they are on vacation Monday
    through Saturday;
and for kids my age who turn handicaps into
    challenges
and tragedies into triumphs.

These may be unsung heroes, Lord,
but do you hear me?
I'm singing their praises now! Amen.

It's a dog's life I'm thanking you for, Lord—
*my* dog's life.

When everyone else is too busy
or too focused on something else,
my dog is still there.
I can count on my dog.
I can be sure of a lick across the face
in the morning
and a leaping greeting when I get home after school.

Please don't take this as a personal criticism,
but when you made cats, you left something out.
Cats are takers.
They're out to get what they can from people.
Dogs, on the other hand, like to give.
They like to slobber all over people,
cuddle up,
and do what brings their masters pleasure.
I'm not a cat-lover, Lord,
but I do love my dog.

Come to think of it,
maybe my dog has a great lesson to teach me—
that giving love and being loyal
bring *my* master pleasure.
You are my master, Lord,
and maybe living a dog's life of love and loyalty
is not a bad idea at all. Amen.

Whenever this girl and I get together, Lord,
I act like a total jerk.
She is good-looking,
no, she is fantastically good-looking,
a lot of fun,
bright,
and, for some strange reason,
I think she likes me.

I, on the other hand,
act like I have air between my ears
whenever I am with her.
I have spilled things,
dropped things,
forgotten things,
and said the wrong things
almost every time I've been with her.

Lord, when does a guy like me
start to be at ease with members of the opposite sex?
The young guys in the movies
always seem to be so smooth and so confident.

I'm not asking, Lord, to make me into a movie star.
Just help me settle down and be myself
because I really do like this girl,
and, for some strange reason,
I really do think she likes me. Amen.

How do I look to others, Lord?
I wish I knew.
I wish I could ask someone—
like the good-looking girl at school
or the guy who is built like a rock
and looks like a movie star.
"How do I look?" I'd like to ask them.
I wonder what they'd say.

I care about how I look, Lord.
It makes a difference.
Sometimes I care too much about how I look.
I get mad at mirrors.
I can get down on myself.
I think I look stupid or plain or different,
and it bothers me.
If I had made me, Lord, the truth is
I might have made a few parts of me different.

Oh, I know.
I can hear you now.
You want me to know that the way you made me
is just the way you want me.
You'd like me to look in a mirror
and say, "There is one good-looking guy."
You'd like me to believe
that anyone made in your image can't be ugly.

Lord, help me appreciate the image in my mirror,
and see it as a reflection of you. Amen.

# ► Save me from stereotypes

Save me from stereotypes, Lord.
Stereotypes say certain people are always a certain way.
You know:
all older people are boring and serious;
all nonathletic people are losers;
all smart people are out of it;
all rich people are happy;
all poor people are lazy.

Stereotypes are not good, Lord.
So I'm asking you to help me when I'm
tempted to lump a whole bunch of people
into one category and label them like
a can of beans or box of cereal.

I'd also like to ask for a special favor:
Give me the courage to break some stereotypes.
Sometimes I think people my age believe
a kid's only worthwhile if you wear
certain clothes, like certain things,
and have certain friends.
I'd like to change that, Lord.
So help me to say yes to the next
chance I get to be different,
to break the mold and maybe change my world.
Amen.

▶ **I like drama**

Lord, I like drama.
I like to be in plays.
Plays help people understand life.
Plays make people laugh, cry, cheer, and
celebrate.

I think you know a lot about drama, Lord.
You know about conflicting characters—
like Jesus and the Pharisees.
You know about surprises—
like a donkey talking!
You know about life—
after all you created it!

So congratulations, Lord, on a good sense of drama.
You must like it, too.
And thanks for the drama you bring to my life—
the characters that march across my life's stage,
the surprises,
the twists in plot,
and the conflicts, too, that work themselves out
into something close to a happy ending.

You're better than Stephen Spielberg, Lord.
People have been talking about your productions
for centuries!
Since we both like drama so much, do you mind
if I ask for a good part in the next school play?
After all, behind every good actor is a great director!
Amen.

There are two words, Lord,
I need to put away in a dark closet
and never use them again:
"I can't."

I fight against being timid, Lord.
I hesitate.
I think I can't measure up,
I tell myself I'll never make it
or that I'm sure to fail.
I get so mad at myself sometimes, Lord.
I defeat myself before I've even tried.

One of your people, the apostle Paul, once wrote,
"I can do all things
through him [Christ] who gives me strength"
    (Philippians 4:13).

I want Paul's confidence, Lord.
Save me from being so timid and so cautious
that I miss opportunities
to do great things for you.

Help me to see that when I say "I can't,"
I'm really saying "I won't" or "I'm afraid."
Then turn me toward you, the king of the universe,
whose power and strength and might
are as close as a prayer. Amen.

## ► **Cleaning up my language**

I'm not sure when it started, Lord,
but my mouth has gotten pretty nasty lately.
I'm using language that a lot of guys use,
and right now, talking to you,
I'm not proud of it at all.

I've thought about why I use bad language.
Here's why, Lord.
(These aren't excuses,
just a way of understanding how and why
my mouth gets so dirty.)
I use bad language
because the people around me do,
and then I feel I fit in and am a part of things.
I use bad language
because it's one way I have
to express my anger, my feelings, and my excitement.
I use bad language
because a lot of people on TV and in movies
use bad language, too.

Lord, I'm asking that by your Spirit
you'll enable me to clean up my language.
I don't need to talk dirty
to prove I'm tough or mature or one of the boys.
I do need to clean up what I say
if I want others to see you—and hear you—
through me. Amen.

► **I have my doubts**

I have my doubts, Lord.
I'll hear something another Christian says
and ask myself, "Do I really believe that?"

Lord, I need help sorting out
what's true and what's false.
I get a lot of mixed signals from people in the church.
I'm left with questions,
and I'm never sure who can give me answers.

I'm OK on the basics, Lord.
I believe I'm a sinner and that Jesus came
to live a perfect life in my place,
to take my punishment on himself,
to die for me,
and to rise to eternal life.
It's on some other things that I have my doubts.

When the doubts come, Lord,
I really need three things.
I need to have some people I can trust
to tell me what they believe and why.
I need to have the gift of deciding
for myself whether what others tell me is true.
And I need to know that even if I have doubts,
you love me and want to hear from me in prayer.
Can I count on you, Lord? Amen.

Somebody, Lord, actually counted
the number of times in the Bible
that this phrase occurs:
"Do not be afraid."
They counted 365 times.
That's one for every day of the year!
Good going, Lord!
You have a clever way of saying
that every fear of every day can be stilled by you.

I do get afraid, Lord.
I'd just as soon not have anyone else know it,
but there are some things that scare me—
like the possibility of a nuclear war,
or losing a member of my family,
or failing a test,
or getting really sick.

In 1 John 4:18, you say,
"Perfect love casts out fear."
When I'm afraid, I need to know
that you love me,
that no matter what happens,
you want for me the highest and the best.
Give me that assurance, Lord,
for every fear of every day. Amen.

Sometimes, Lord, when I think about my family,
I start saying all these sentences
that begin with the words, "I wish I had. . . ."

I wish I had a bigger room.
I wish I had a dad who did more things with me.
I wish I had a house with a swimming pool.
I wish I had a nicer family car.
I wish I had a big-screen TV
and a lifelong, unlimited membership
in a video club.
I wish I had permission to stay out as late
as I want to.
I wish I had a brother or sister who
didn't terrorize my life.
I wish I had a church that had services
at one o'clock on Sunday afternoons
that lasted for, say, 15 minutes max.
Then I wouldn't get hassled
about getting up on Sunday mornings
and staying awake during worship.

Lord, I'm always looking for something more.
Help me to be content, Lord.
Help me celebrate a family that loves me
and wants the best for me.
Help me celebrate how blessed I am—
even at eight o'clock on Sunday morning. Amen.

# ► How important can one person be?

Do you remember a man named Telemachus, Lord?
Of course you do.
You keep track of everybody.

In the days when gladiators fought
in the arenas of the Roman empire,
Telemachus, an Asian monk,
came to the Colosseum in Rome and was shocked
to see crowds cheer for the killing of a human being.
So Telemachus stood up and shouted,
"In the name of the Lord Jesus,
let the killing cease!"
They booed him. They knocked him over.
Still he shouted,
"In the name of the Lord Jesus,
let the killing cease!"
Finally, someone ran a sword through him,
but the courageous monk died shouting,
"In the name of the Lord Jesus,
let the killing cease!"
Legend says, Lord, that after Telemachus died,
people left the Colosseum silently
and never returned again to see a gladiators' contest.

Lord, when I feel that I'm not very important
or that my life may not amount to much,
give me the courage and the confidence of Telemachus
to stand up for what I believe
and to make a difference in my world. Amen.

Something has to change, Lord.
Lately, I've been down on just about everything.
If someone held up a glass of water and asked,
"Is the glass half-full or half-empty?"
do you know what I'd say, Lord?
I'd say, "Who cares about the dumb glass, anyway!"

Something is wrong, Lord.
I don't understand it,
but if I were the people closest to me,
I don't think I'd like me very much.

What really gets me mad about this
is that I can't seem to break out of it.
I feel bad about things and expect the worst,
and because I expect the worst, the worst happens,
and then I feel even worse than before!

Lord, I need a change in attitude.
I need someone to cheer me up.
I need an event or an activity
that will turn me around.

I'm talking to you, Lord, because you know
that I'm not doing much with my life right now
and that I'm up against a dead end.
I'm talking to you
because you know how to do a miracle. Amen.

# ▶ Patience, Lord, I need patience

I have a list, Lord.
It's a list of things at home
that drive me crazy.

Here goes . . .
people smacking their lips when they eat;
family members who steal my hair dryer;
adults telling me to turn down the volume;
parents who ask too many questions at supper;
people getting upset about dumb little things
like what TV show to watch
and who gets to sit in what chair;
a parent forcing me to go someplace
where I really don't want to go;
a brother or sister competing for
the "All-American Whiner Award."

Lord, all of these things drive me crazy,
and the list goes on.
So when my blood starts to boil,
and the hair on the back of my neck
begins to curl,
and I feel as if a nuclear test is being staged
inside my body,
when I'm ready to blow, shout, scream,
and erupt like a volcano,
then, Lord, give me patience. Amen.

Lord, I can't wait to drive.
Getting my license will mean being able to go
where I want to go
without having to ask for a ride.
I'll feel more grown-up and responsible.
I'll be free.

Before I get my license, Lord, I'd like to make
a few promises.
I promise that I'll recognize how powerful a car can be.
A car does more than just move people from place to
place.
A car can hurt and kill.

I promise, too, Lord,
that I won't use my driving to impress people
with my willingness to break the law
or my courage to drive at fast speeds.

Another promise I want to make is this:
Lord, I will never mix drinking and driving.
Too many people not much older than I
are dying on highways because they were driving
drunk.
I know that makes you sad, Lord.
I won't be a part of it. I promise.

Thank you, Lord, for the privilege of driving.
When I get behind the wheel, I'll remember what I've
promised.
Honest. Amen.

I hate the word, Lord—
*suicide*.
When people my age commit suicide,
do they really want to die?
I mean, do they believe that dying is better than
living?

I've been really down sometimes, Lord.
It was like being alone in a dark room.
I felt empty inside
and hurt
and very confused.

Then something happened.
You were there, Lord, just as you're here now,
and I felt your love.
You gave me people to listen and to understand.
I gave it time,
and, sure enough, tomorrow looked better.

Lord, I'm praying for everyone my age
who faces darkness alone.
Come to them, Lord, as you've come to me.
Help me to see the hurts in people close to me.
Help me to care enough about others to say
"Tomorrow will be a better day." Amen.

# ▶ Friendship Prayers ◀

There's something I have to admit, Lord.
It's a part of me I don't like very much.
Something tells me you're not too crazy about it,
    either.

Whenever I meet somebody new,
especially someone I really want to get close to,
I pretend I'm someone else.
It's not that I lie, well,
maybe it is sort of a lie.
I stretch my accomplishments.
I try to create an image that I'm someone
bigger and better than I am.

It's not that I claim to be a personal friend
of Sylvester Stallone or anything.
I just try to look too good,
better than "true good," if you know what I mean.

I think you called this hypocrisy
in the Bible, Lord.
You've always loved hypocrites, I know,
but you've always wanted them to love themselves
enough to celebrate who they were in you.

So next time I meet a potential friend,
help me to leave my mask at home
and be me.
Even you'd have to agree, Lord,
there is no one else quite like me. Right? Amen.

# ► Some friends ask too much

I'm having a hard time with a friend, Lord,
who asks too much of me.
It's sort of like I want this friend
to have a part in the drama of my life,
but my friend wants to have the starring role.

Sometimes I feel almost as if
my friend owns me.
It's as if I can't do anything,
or go anyplace,
or make any decision
without having this friend be a part of it.

I need breathing room, Lord,
I need some space.
My problem is this:
How do I get the space I need
and still keep my friendship?
How do I let my friend know
that I'd like to have a few other friends
and do a few things on my own?
How can I do this without hurting feelings
or ending up with a broken friendship?

Give me the right words to say
and the courage to say them.
I want to speak the truth
and I want to speak it in love.
So, Lord, could I ask for a little inspiration? Amen.

# ▶ For the put-down artist

Nobody, I mean, nobody,
can put people down like this friend of mine.
This friend uses words like a chain saw,
Cutting people down to where they feel like sawdust.

I've thought about put-down artists, Lord.
I remember how King David in the Old Testament
ran into a guy who kept hurling insults at him.
The guy's name was Shimei.

Lord, I'm praying for this Shimei I know
and every other Shimei
who's ever put another person down.
Somehow, Lord, help them
(or maybe I should say help *us*)
to understand an important truth:
When we put others down
we're really just saying
that we don't think much of ourselves.

Help us to feel so good about ourselves
and about your love for us and for all people
that we build others up
instead of tearing them down.

Lord, we could use fewer Shimeis and chain saws
and a lot more love. Amen.

# ▶ My friend is in the hospital

I don't know much about hospitals, Lord.
I know they're clean—very clean.
I know the best place you can be when you're sick
is in the hospital.
I also know if I were in the hospital,
I'd be afraid,
uncertain,
and definitely worried.

So, Lord, as I think about my friend
in the hospital,
I'm asking most of all that you'll make him better.
Help out the doctors and nurses
and when a little extra is called for—
you know, something beyond their regular, everyday
  skills—
be there for them, Lord,
so that they can be there for my friend.

There's something more, Lord.
If my friend thinks about the hospital as I do
and feels what I'd feel inside,
then bring these special gifts—
peace, courage, confidence, and endurance.
Maybe, Lord, I can help a little, too,
with a visit, a card, and the right words
at the right time.
I'll give it a try. Amen.

# ▶ I have a friend who's really down

Have you heard of the dipper and the bucket, Lord?
I'm sure you have.
You've heard about everything.

Anyway, there is this psychologist, Dr. Clifton,
who says that everybody has a dipper and a bucket.
He says we all walk around with a bucket.
It gets filled when people encourage us
and build us up.
It gets emptied when people criticize us
and put us down.
Sometimes we empty our buckets ourselves.

Well, Lord, I'm praying for a friend
whose bucket needs filling.
Quite a few people, I think,
have had their dippers in my friend's bucket.
This friend is running on empty, Lord.

So help me to fill my friend's bucket
with an honest compliment
and a word or a look of encouragement that says,
"You are my friend.
I admire you.
You're gifted.
You're not a nobody.
You're a person who deserves
to have your bucket filled." Amen.

# ▶ Where do we get help, Lord?

Today, Lord, I'm praying for a friend
who has a serious problem.

This friend's problem is a big one, Lord.
It's the kind that makes some kids
get really down and do something dumb—
like run away
or hurt someone
or hurt themselves.

Lord, when people our age hurt like this,
where do we get help?
I didn't know what to say or to do.
Do pastors know what we feel inside, Lord?
Do school counselors understand us?
What about our parents, Lord, and our grandparents?
Can we trust them to listen to us
and love us
even if what we tell them
is more than we can handle?

I hope so, Lord.
I hope all these adults who say they care so much
really do care
because my friend and a whole lot of other kids
really need to know they're not alone.
Give my friend someone, Lord, beginning with me.
Amen.

# ► **My friend is moving away**

So how do you keep a friendship going
when your friend moves away?
I know, Lord.
Write letters.
Make phone calls.
Send Christmas presents.
It is possible, isn't it?

Come to think of it, Lord,
you and I are good friends,
and we're pretty far apart sometimes, aren't we?
I mean—you're in heaven
and I'm on earth.
Wait a minute, though.
You also said you would be with me always,
that you would never leave me.

Jesus said he is with us always.
As I understand it,
Jesus can be everywhere at once.
I wish I could.
It's really something, though.
Christ is with me now,
and Christ is with my friend at the same time,
no matter where we move.
I like that.
If Christ is with me and Christ is with my friend,
then, Lord, we must be together—in Christ!
One in Christ. I do like that. Amen.

I've decided, Lord, that I don't like fights.
I have a friend who is mad at me,
and we're each waiting for the other
to apologize,
get down on one's knees,
cower a little
and admit what a terrible mistake was made.

Something tells me, Lord, that isn't going to happen.
So I'm asking you for some help.
Give me the willingness to take the first step
toward making this right.
Help me not to put this off too long.
I know that letting a fight go on
can lead to resentment, bitterness, and even hatred.

This is my friend, Lord.
How could I forget that?
I really do want to get back on track
with this valuable person in my life.
So, Lord, turn us both around
to face you
and to face each other.

You're a master when it comes to forgiveness.
I suppose that's why I came to you. Amen.

# ► My friend's parents are getting divorced

Divorce hurts, Lord.
I don't know what it's like to fall in love,
get married,
and spend a lot of years together,
and then decide to split
and live your lives apart.

It must hurt.
I know it hurts my friend.
I can tell.
We kids like things tight and secure and happy.
I like things to be predictable, Lord.
My friend does, too.

So it hurts to see a family change,
especially when the family is yours.
It hurts when parents don't get along
and almost make their kids choose sides.

Lord, help me to bring some security to my friend.
I want my friend to know
that I'm a sure thing,
that I can be counted on to be there,
and that you can be counted on, too.

Help my friend's friendship with me
and faith in you
be two sure things. Amen.

# ▶ What do you say when a friend's parent dies?

What do you say, Lord,
when a friend's parent dies?

I know it must hurt way down deep.
I've worried sometimes about one of my parents dying.
I wonder, Lord, what I'd want people to say to me
at a time like this.

I know a lot of people say,
"Receive my sympathy."
I don't think I can say that.
It doesn't sound very real or sincere.
It's just not something I'd say.

Lord, I remember when Jesus' good friend Lazarus
    died.
In the shortest verse of the whole Bible
it says, "Jesus wept."
Your Son cried, Lord.
He cried because he hurt inside,
and he cried because others hurt, too.

Right now, Lord, I feel what my friend feels.
I really do.
I know how much this parent will be missed.
I can imagine the fear, the sadness, and the tears.

So, Lord, help me to say what I feel,
and if the words don't come,
at least help me to show that I care. Amen.

# ▶ **Family Prayers** ◀

▶ **The family that laughs together**

Sometimes, Lord, I worry about our family.
Everyone is so busy. We're not together enough.
So today I'm praying that we can have more fun
as a family.

We've had some great times in the past, Lord.
Supper can be a real blast.
Somebody starts giggling during grace
(sorry about that),
and pretty soon we're all cracking up.
Or someone tells a joke with a crazy punch line,
and one of us laughs so hard,
she falls off her chair
or sends her mashed potatoes across the table.

I love times like that, Lord.
I think I like our family best
when we're laughing.
So please give us more time for laughter.
Please help us to slow down.
Help us use laughter as a sign
that we love to be together.

I heard somebody say that
"laughter is the best medicine."
So, Lord, please fill this prescription.
I think we'd all feel better about things at home
if we'd laugh a little more.
I know I would. Amen.

► **I want to say what I feel**

I don't know why, Lord,
but sometimes I just won't say what I feel.
I know it really bugs the people in my home.

I'll come home looking like my best friend died.
My chin will be on my chest,
and I'll have sorrow written all over me.
Then my parent will say,
"Hey, you look terrible. Is anything wrong?"
And I'll say, "Nope. Everything's fine."
Why do I do that, Lord?
Why do I hide my feelings
from those who love me most?

I really do want to say what I feel.
So why don't I?
I think maybe it's because
I don't believe they'll understand me
or because I'm sure they'll think I'm stupid or
    overreacting.

Lord, I have to trust people more,
especially the people in my family.
I really do need these people.
I need you, too.
I can't go it alone.
I have to believe that, like you,
the people in my home care about what I feel inside
and want to understand. Amen.

## ► My parents are good people

Sometimes, Lord, I say things I don't mean.
This is especially true when I think about my parents.

I can get all upset and think the worst about them.
I'll think they don't care about my feelings.
I'll think they're cold and insensitive.
I'll tell myself that they don't even want
to understand me.
I'll wonder what it would be like
to have Bill Cosby for a dad
or to live on my own on some island
or at least someplace where there would be a sign,
"Parents, keep off."

Then something happens.
I think you make it happen, Lord.
It's one of your ways of bringing us back
to what's real and true and accurate.
My parent says something really right on target.
My parent looks at me in a way that says,
"I'm proud of you. I love you."
Then it dawns on me—parents really do care.
They really do want the highest and the best for me.
And that's love.
My parents are good people, Lord.
With your help, I'll remember that. Amen.

## ► Thanks for my grandparents

Lord, I think I know why
you put grandparents in my life.
You know I need
someone who laughs at my jokes
even when they aren't funny;
someone who knows what life was like
before music videos;
someone who can hear the word *apple*
and think of a tree before a computer;
someone who finds a lot of pleasure
in being proud of me.

Thank you, Lord, for my grandparents,
for the way they give my life roots
and history
and a connection between now
and what used to be.

Sometime soon, Lord, while there still is time,
give me the courage to say to my grandparents:
"My life is better and richer because of you.
You may not always understand this grandson of yours,
but this grandson of yours loves you very much."
Amen.

► **Cain and Abel revisited**

It's no wonder, Lord, that the first murder in history
came during a fight between brothers.
From the very beginning,
brothers and sisters had a hard time getting along.

I've been thinking about this.
What causes brothers and sisters to fight so much?
It's the same, old problem, Lord,
the same old thing—sin.
We brothers and sisters fight because of sin.
Sin has as many faces in our relationships
as brothers and sisters in families.
Sin comes as jealousy,
greed,
insensitivity,
hurtful anger,
harmful teasing,
and lies that put others down and
make them look bad.

Lord, I'm asking for your Spirit to help me
when I'm about to cause another fight
with my brother or sister.
When I'm about ready to say the bad thing
or to get nasty and rude,
when I'm ready to be the Rambo of our house,
stop me in my tracks
and teach me that being a brother
means going out of my way
to make peace, not war. Amen.

I don't want anybody else to hear—
at least not quite yet, Lord.
I've been thinking about how little I do
around the house.
It isn't hard to think about it.
I am reminded of it almost every day
by somebody at home.

Between you and me, Lord,
I'm wondering (just wondering)
what I could do to make things a little easier
for the rest of the family.
Now, I said, I'm just wondering.
I'd hate to have the family think
I was about to volunteer for cleaning the bathroom
every day.
I'm not.

I wonder, though, what I could do around the house.
It should be something simple at first, I suppose,
a promise I could make and keep—
like taking out the garbage,
or hanging up my clothes,
or putting the dishes in the dishwasher once a week—
something I can just do without a lot of fuss.

I'll wonder about this some more, Lord.
Then help me to decide and to follow through. Amen.

# ► Before and After ◄
# Prayers

It's a brand new day, Lord.
Yesterday's mistakes and failures are behind me,
separated by a night of sleep and rest.
I want to start today right—
with good things on my mind.
So you're on my mind, Lord, right at the start.

I begin today thanking you
that you've decided to give me this day as a gift.
I'll make the most of it, I promise.
I'm thankful, too, that you'll be with me
in whatever I face today,
using the people and events of my life
to make me into a stronger Christian.

I know a lot of what's ahead of me today, Lord.
I have some planned activities
and a schedule to keep.
I also know there will be some surprises,
things I'd never expect that will make my day
different and unique from every other day of my life.

This day will be the best of days, Lord,
as you bless me with someone to serve
and with a chance to love others as you love me.
It's a good, good day, Lord,
as I begin it with thoughts of you. Amen.

When night comes, Lord,
I think of all the people who work at night,
people like police officers, nurses, and firefighters.
While I'm asleep, they're taking care of things.

You're like that, Lord.
Since I was very young, I've fallen asleep
feeling safe and secure with you still awake,
watching over the whole world,
sending angels out on assignment
to guard us waking and guard us sleeping.

Every time I fall asleep, Lord,
it's a little bit like dying.
I enter darkness
only to wake up again to the light of a new day.
Through it all, the darkness and the light,
you're still at work, on the job,
looking out for me.

As this day ends, Lord, thanks for always being there,
24 hours a day, 365 days a year,
with an extra day during leap year.
What long hours you keep, Lord!
Thanks for keeping them with me.
Good night until the morning, Lord. Amen.

You and I both know, Lord,
that I'm not crazy about tests.
Maybe I've been burned once too often.
I study one way, and the test goes another.
I misunderstand directions and lose 20 points.
I think I'm ready, and I'm not. We get our papers
back and I make sure
no one else sees my paper
with the embarrassing score.

Lord, I'm not asking for a miracle on this test.
I'm not even asking for a perfect paper
(although if there is a chance . . . ).
I am asking, though, that you'll watch over me.
Save me from dumb mistakes.
Save me from drawing a blank on stuff I knew
just last night.
Save me from getting so uptight
that I can't really show what I've learned.
And, Lord, save me from thinking I'm a failure
just because I fail to answer something right
on this test.

Maybe tests are important, Lord.
Maybe a test at school—like this one—
will help me face the big tests of life
still to come.
I'm glad we can face together this test
and the tests to come. Amen.

### If you did well

I bet, Lord, you didn't expect to hear from me.
It seems whenever I do well
I forget to say thanks.
Not this time, Lord.
I know I came through on this test
because I prepared well
and because I knew you were there helping me.
So thank you.

Could it be that you're sort of like my parent
who gets that look of pleasure
whenever I do my best?
I hope so . . . Father. Amen.

### If you did poorly

Choke!
Lord, I feel terrible about this test. I blew it.
I'm embarrassed, angry, and disappointed.
Help me to take something positive
away from this experience.
Help me to study harder next time,
to ask questions about what I didn't understand,
and to realize that life goes on
after blowing a test.
I know you love me no matter how I do on tests.
Right now I need that. Amen.

When I was little, Lord, I'd listen to a story
about a kid named Alexander who had a terrible,
horrible, no good, very bad day.
Everything that could have gone wrong in his day did.

Something tells me this is going to be
one of those days.
I really don't want to feel this way
about the day ahead. I just do.
So I need your help.

Here in this prayer, Lord, I want to tell you
how much I need what you've promised to give me—
your power,
your guidance,
confidence in my gifts and my goals,
angels to watch over me,
your Spirit to inspire and lead me,
and a peace deep inside of me
that says things really are going to be OK.

A lot could go wrong today, Lord.
Help me to think about what could go right,
especially when I lean on you. Amen.

Now the day is over, Lord.
It's almost like a curtain
coming down at the end of a play.
Or it's like a book way at the end
where the last page is blank, empty, and white.

This has been a hard day.
The big things I worried about are behind me.
Finally, no one is expecting me to perform
or to excel or to meet the deadline
or to do the hard things.
Now it's you and I, Lord, just talking.

I remember reading in the Bible
how Jesus used to have tough days.
He would get away from the crowds,
wander off alone someplace,
and pray.
Then he would find the strength he needed
to do it all again.

Tough days like this one, Lord,
teach me that I can't do life alone.
I really do need you.
I'm no master of the universe or superhero
or any of the other heroic characters
I used to enjoy when I was younger.
I'm just myself, and I have you with me,
and together we made it through today. Thanks.
Amen.

It's a big game, Lord, and I can feel it.
Inside of me is a whole flock of butterflies,
and they're not flying in formation, either.
I have a lot of questions:
Am I ready?
What if I do something stupid?
If I lose, can I handle it?
Can I handle it if we win?

O Lord, I don't even want to think about losing.
I want to win.
So I have a big question for you—
Whose side are you on, anyway?
Are you pulling for us or for them, Lord?

Somebody told me once that you don't choose sides.
Is that true, Lord?
Is it true that all you want for every one of us
is that we do our best?
If that's the way it is, Lord,
then help me to do my best.
In fact, help us all to do our best,
our team and theirs.

Win or lose, Lord, I'd like to play this game
in your honor.
Thanks for the gifts you've given me
that allow me to begin this game with confidence.
Amen.

► **After winning a game**

We did it! Lord, I love to win!
I worried. I doubted. I did my best. Then we won!
Wow! Winning feels good!
It's as if the whole world stands up and shouts,
"There's a winner!"

I wonder if people remember winners very long.
Let's see—
Who won the World Series three years ago?
Who won the Superbowl in 1983?
I hope people remember this. I hope I do, too.

It's quiet now, Lord. I have some time to think
and to talk with you.
Sometimes I love winning so much that I forget
about those who lost and those who hardly ever win.
Sometimes I forget that the difference
between winning and losing
can be a single error, one bad mistake, or a bad call.
Winning, Lord, is a fragile thing.

Lord, make me a good winner.
Help me to show kindness to those who feel defeated.
Help me to be humble when I get compliments.
Help me do what you do so well—
make others feel like winners every day!

Thanks for this moment, Lord.
I'll cherish it, celebrate it, and remember it
for a long time. Amen.

Well, Lord, it's over.
They won, and we lost.
I feel angry about some things, sad about others.
I wonder if I could have tried harder.

The thing about losing that really gets me, Lord,
is that losing is so final.
You don't get a second chance.
There always are two locker rooms just like on TV.
One has a party.
The other has a funeral.

I do wonder, Lord, why you made a world
in which people have to win or lose.
Is it to show us that here on earth
we can never have it all,
that there is only one place where we'll be
completely and forever winners,
and that's heaven?

I like your idea of heaven, Lord.
It sounds like a great place, especially today.
It will be great to wear the winner's crown
every day in heaven.

Maybe every time we lose you teach us something.
Is that it, Lord?
One thing's for sure:
When I talk to you, I don't feel like a loser. Amen.

# ► Prayers for Big ◄
# Days

► **On my birthday**

So here I am, Lord,
another year older.
I used to wonder what it would be like
to be this age.
Now I know
and, honestly, I don't feel any different.

Looking ahead, Lord, the age of 20 seems pretty old.
I have a hard time imagining myself at 30 or 40 or 50.
I wish I knew how long I'd live.
It would sure make life a little easier.
On the other hand, it would also make life
much less exciting.
Maybe it's best if I just live for today
and not worry about tomorrow.
Didn't you say something about that once, Lord?

Thank you for watching over me
during this year of my life, Lord.
Thank you for always being there
even when I didn't notice you or talk with you.
It's really good to know that you remember
what it's like to be my age.
A lot of things may change this next year,
but you and I are solid, Lord. Solid. Amen.

# ▶ On the first day of a new school year

It's a new school year, Lord.
Summer's over.
Thanks for all the great times I had.
Thanks, too, for the summer days
that weren't all that great.

Now it's back to school.
I'd like people to think I'm all ready
to make top grades,
star in sports,
and maybe even be a success with the girls.
You can see right through me, though,
can't you, Lord?

I'm nervous.
I'm not as sure of myself
as I want others to believe.
So, Lord, give me the wisdom to ask questions
when I'm not sure what happens next.
Give me the honesty to say, "I don't know,"
when I'm asked a tough question.
Most of all, give me the vision to see a good year
    ahead,
recognizing that a good year is what you want for me,
and that seeing it now, in prayer, ahead of time,
will help make a good year possible. Amen.

There is this play, called *Our Town*.
I know you like drama, Lord.
I'm sure you know about this play.
In one scene a girl named Emily has died,
and she is given permission
to relive one day of her life.
She returns to earth, invisible,
and takes in all the beauty of an ordinary day.
What's amazing, Lord, is that it was too much for her.
She said she couldn't handle it.
It was too rich.

I'm thankful, Lord, for the richest blessings
of the most ordinary day.
On this Thanksgiving Day, receive my thanks
for the smell of good things cooking in the kitchen,
for the laughs that echo around our house,
for the way people in my home,
and my town, and my country
pitch in to make life beautiful and rich
and sometimes almost too much to take in.

Thank you, Lord, that I live in a nation
where ordinary days are blessed by you
with the extraordinary gifts
of liberty and justice. Amen.

How do you celebrate Christmas in heaven, Lord?
Is there some sort of cosmic light show?
Or do you light up stars a million light years away
for you and the angels to see?
Do the angels put on a Christmas concert, Lord?
Do you gather everybody in heaven around you
and tell them what it was like when you were on
    earth?

If you ask me, Lord,
Christmas is a time when we earthlings
get pretty close to heaven.
Do you remember goose bumps, Lord?
You did get goose bumps on earth, didn't you?
It's not the sort of thing I tell others about,
but I will tell you—
I get goose bumps this time of year.
The carols and the beautiful story of your birth,
the traditions we have at home
and the way everybody tries to be friendlier.
I love it all, Lord. It's like heaven comes to earth.
Even from heaven, we must look just about our best
at Christmas.
Wouldn't you agree?

So merry Christmas, Lord! And happy birthday!
Maybe the distance between way up there
and way down here
isn't quite as huge this time of year. Amen.

Lord Jesus, there are certain things I believe because
    of Easter,
and I want you to know that I believe them.

I believe that you died a real death,
that when they took you down from the cross,
you were as dead as the people buried in cemeteries.
I believe that you came alive after death,
surprising everybody with that miracle.
I believe when you promised,
"Because I live you shall live also,"
you were talking to me
and to everyone who believes in you.
I believe that because of your resurrection,
there always is hope,
even for people who are really depressed,
even for people who think
that the end of their story is written,
and that it ends in tragedy and death.

More than anything, Lord, I'm grateful
that you have given me and every Christian
a life story with a happy ending—
a story that ends and begins all over again in heaven.
I know the beginning of my life story, Lord,
and I know the ending, too.
But I'm still working on the middle. Amen.

Lord, I am ready for a break.
I know you understand the need we human beings have
to shut down the engines for a while
and just park.
You rested on the seventh day.
Remember, Lord?
I'm glad you did.
I'm glad you rested.
Now it's my turn.

During this break, Lord,
give me enough time to relax,
to be with my friends,
to put my feet up and do nothing
(and not get hassled for it),
and to stay up late without worrying about
what time I have to get up.

I need this break, Lord.
I was starting to get pretty nasty.
I was tired,
and when that happens,
I say things I don't mean
and get into trouble.

Lord, on the other end of this break
I want to feel fresh and new
and ready to go at it again.
So help me to make the most of this break.
Help me to rest. Amen.

I've never been crazy about endings, Lord.
Beginnings are much more fun.
I want to take a minute here to look back
at the school year that's ending.
This is sort of our secret, Lord,
sort of our personal yearbook.

Maybe our yearbook, Lord, would look a little
different
from the usual yearbook.
I know that learning and awards and fun
are all important to you,
but maybe our yearbook would include
some other pictures like these:
the kid with cancer who kept coming to school,
the guy who stuck up for the one
who was always being put down,
the girl who said no to drugs three times,
the teacher who talked about his deepest feelings
in front of the class;
and the football player who turned and walked away
when he got shoved during the big game.

As I remember this school year, Lord,
I'm thankful for the stuff that's in both yearbooks—the
one they publish at school
and the one that's just between us. Amen.

# ► Prayers about People in the Bible ◄ and Me

► **Zacchaeus**

*Read Luke 19:1-10.*

Lord Jesus, have you noticed me,
little old, ordinary me?
Like Zacchaeus, I'm up a tree
watching you from a distance.

Zacchaeus wanted to see you, Lord,
but he also wanted to keep his distance.
He wanted to get a look at you,
but he also wanted to keep on robbing people blind
as a rich tax collector.

I'm a lot like Zacchaeus.
I watch you from a distance, Lord,
close enough to see you,
but far enough away to keep up my bad habits
and my "favorite" sins.

You surprised Zacchaeus, Lord.
You surprised him right out of his tree.
You invited yourself to his home for dinner
and changed him from the inside out.

Surprise me, Lord. Shake me up. Call my name.
Come close, Lord. Come home for dinner.
I've been up a tree too long. Amen.

► **The rich young man**

*Read Matthew 19:16-22.*

Here was a guy who had all the right answers, Lord.
He was a religious whiz kid
and a rich one at that!
You sure caught him by surprise
when you said that, if he was serious about eternal
    life,
he'd have to give up all he owned to the poor.

It makes me wonder, Lord.
What would you have expected me to give up
if I were the rich young man?
Everything?
Or just my stereo,
or my skis,
or my bike,
or my next vacation?

Some things do get in the way, Lord, don't they?
That's what you wanted that rich young man to
    know—
that he could be a pretty good person
and still be in trouble spiritually.
Here was a religious guy who never had to sacrifice
or to serve,
or to decide which is more important:
the things he owned or you.

Who are the rich young men today, Lord?
Could I be one of them? Amen.

## ▶ The boy with a little that turned into a lot

*Read John 6:1-15.*

So, Lord, how did he rate?
This little guy comes up with a little bread and some
    fish,
and you make a miracle.
You fed 5000 people from that little bit.

Sometimes I wish you would make more of me.
I feel pretty small sometimes.
Oh, I know, people keep telling me
that my day will come.
I just wish my day was today.
That's all.

I keep hearing people at church say
that my friends and I are the future of the church.
That's nice of them to say, all right.
I just wish they saw us as the present of the church,
    too.
You know,
the way you saw that boy with the bread and fish
as a kid worthy to participate in your miracle.

I'm asking, Lord, that people in the church
start taking us older kids seriously.
I guess I'm asking that you help them respect us more
and maybe expect more out of us.
If they do, and I hope they do,

we'll be there for them
the way that boy with the bread and fish was there for
  you. Amen.

*Read Mark 14:66-72.*

Why do I pretend sometimes, Lord,
that I don't know you?
Why do I want people to think
that I don't really take you very seriously?
What am I afraid of, Lord?

Peter was afraid that if people knew he was your
    disciple,
he would be imprisoned or even killed.
So he pretended he didn't know you.
He put up a hard front,
used tough language,
and, sure enough, he looked and sounded like, well,
someone who didn't know you.

I need courage, Lord.
I need to feel confident in my relationship with you.
How could I ever be ashamed of you, Lord?
You love me.
You died for me.
You did it all for me, Lord.
Give me the courage to be honest and open
about my feelings toward you,
especially when I'm tempted to deny
that you and I are best friends. Amen.

# Old man Zebedee

*Read Matthew 4:18-22.*

This prayer isn't about Peter or Andrew, Lord,
and it isn't about James and John.
It's about the guy who raised James and John,
the owner of Zebedee and Sons, Fishing Enterprises,
   Inc.

I'm just curious, Lord.
Why did Zebedee decide to stay home and fish
while his two sons went with Jesus?
What was with Zebedee, anyway?
Couldn't the guy see that by staying with the boat
he was missing the boat?

How could he miss such a great opportunity?
Let me guess—
he was greedy and wanted to keep his business;
he was old and couldn't hit the road
with a traveling teacher;
or maybe he was too stuck in his ways
to follow a dream.

You know what I hope, Lord?
I hope Zebedee eventually followed you.
I hope, too, that when I'm older
and you call me to a challenge or adventure,
I'll be ready to go,
hook, line, and sinker. Amen.

► **John Mark**

*Read Mark 14:51-52; Acts 15:36-41; and 2 Timothy 4:11.*

Lord, I just took a close look at your servant, John
    Mark.
They also called him just plain Mark.
Anyway, word has it he was the guy
who ran out of the Garden of Gethsemane
without his pajamas. Right?

Word also has it that on Paul's first missionary trip,
John Mark got homesick and ran home to mom.
That caused quite an argument between Paul
and his friend, Barnabas, when Barnabas wanted Paul
to take Mark on another trip.

Then, Lord, near the end of Paul's life,
John Mark was labeled by Paul as "useful."

If you ask me, Lord, John Mark was not exactly
your consistent servant.
He had his good days and his bad days.
He was a failure at serving you sometimes,
and at other times he was a real winner.

John Mark and I have a lot in common.
Lord, you know I can really let you down sometimes.
I want you to know, though, that even if I fail,
I hope you'll call on me again,
and maybe in the end, like Mark,
there will be a gospel according to me. Amen.

*Read Acts 9:10-19.*

Sometimes, Lord—you have to admit—
you ask a lot.
Here was Saul, a certified Christian killer,
now blinded after his conversion on the road to
    Damascus.
And here was Ananias, Mr. Average Christian,
being told by you to go and pay a friendly visit on
    Saul,
lay his hands on the guy,
and help him to see again.

Lord, how could you expect that of Ananias?
I'm not sure I would have gone.
What a guy—Ananias!
He found Saul, put his arm around him
and called him "brother"!
You have a way, Lord, of making people do the
    impossible.

I've got some people in my life, Lord,
who make me afraid inside, uncertain, and cautious.
They threaten me and intimidate me.
They're blind to what I feel inside about them.
They don't see me for who I really am.

I'd just as soon have nothing to do with them, Lord,

but maybe, just maybe, considering the courage of
   Ananias,
maybe I can find a reason—with these Sauls of mine—
to call them "brother" or "sister."
It's worth a try. Amen.

► **Barnabas**

*Read Acts 4:36-37.*

I don't think I'd ever want to name a son of mine
    Barnabas,
but, Lord, I do like the meaning of that name.
Barnabas means, "son of encouragement."

Everybody needs encouragement, Lord.
The more sons and daughters of encouragement we
    have,
the better off we are.

I thank you, Lord, for each and every Barnabas in my
    life—
the parent with the compliment,
the coach with the spark to light my fire, and
the teacher with the note at the top of the page.
I thank you for people who make me believe in myself
and in my gifts.
I'm grateful for the words of encouragement like,
"Good job!"
and "Well done!"
and "You can do it!"
and "Go for it!"

There are people in life, Lord, who light up a room
just by walking into it.
I see them and talk to them,
and I hold my head higher.
They are Barnabas to me, a gift from you. Amen.

*Read Philippians 2:25-29.*

I can hardly say his name, Lord.
Epaphroditus.
He was with Paul for just a short time.
Then he got sick and had to go home to Philippi.
Paul appreciated him, though,
even though he could help only for just a little while.

Lord, I'd like to thank you for every Epaphroditus
in my life,
everyone who may stay in my life story for only a little
   while,
but who leaves me a better person.

Thank you for teachers who had me in class for a year
and who had to say good-bye when the school year ended.
Thank you for the friend who brought good times
and then had to move away.
Thank you for actors, musicians, athletes, dancers,
   directors,
and everyone
who, in one great performance,
stirs my spirit
and helps me soar and discover
things about myself and about life
that I have never seen before.

Epaphroditus lives, Lord, in my life,
and I'm thankful. Amen.

► **Eutychus**

*Read Acts 20:7-12.*

Lord, I thank you for including Eutychus [YOU-ti-
    cuss]
in your story of the early church.
Here was a guy who just couldn't stay awake
during one of Paul's sermons.
Unfortunately, when he fell asleep,
he also fell out of the third story window and died.
You raised him from the dead, though,
and, at least the way the story reads,
Paul decided to say "Amen!" and end his sermon.

Like Eutychus, Lord,
I can get very sleepy in church,
especially when the sermon goes too long
or over my head.
I hope you don't take it personally.
I know it isn't right.
I really do like to listen to somebody preach about you
but it has to be someone who gets excited about you
and makes it interesting.
I know you'd like me to listen well
no matter who is preaching or for how long.
I will work at that, Lord.
For now, thanks for raising Eutychus from the dead
after he fell asleep.
I'd hate to think falling asleep in church was fatal.
Amen.

*Read Romans 16:22.*

Who was this guy, Tertius, Lord?
And how does he deserve a verse in the Bible?
It looks like he wrote down the letter for Paul
as Paul dictated his inspired message.
Is that it, Lord?
Was Tertius sort of a secretary?

I wonder if Paul knew that Tertius added his little
hello
to the book of Romans.
You knew, though, didn't you, Lord?
So why did you give this guy his verse?
Why all these hundreds of years later
does Tertius get his name in print—
in the Bible, no less?

Maybe Tertius represents everybody in the church
who does little things
with very little reward.
Maybe you want us younger people to know
that you do appreciate
when we wash windows at church,
when we fold bulletins,
and when we help out with the church nursery.

So Tertius got to say hello. Nice touch, Lord. Amen.

# ► Prayers on the Lord's Prayer ◄

► **Our Father who art in heaven**

I thank you, Lord, that you are in heaven.
It makes me feel secure to know
that you are on top of things.

I thank you, too, that the Lord's Prayer
is for Christians to speak together.
There are no words like *I,* and *me,* and *my*
in this prayer;
only *we,* and *us,* and *our.*
This prayer, Lord, helps me celebrate my oneness
with everyone who has faith in you.

I'm grateful, too, that I can call you Father.
I feel like a celebrity when I talk to you, Lord.
I feel like the son of a famous person
who can talk every day to a history maker.
That's you, Lord, a history maker,
and here we are, talking like a parent and a son.

You are my parent, Lord.
You care about me.
You provide for me.
You want the best for me.
You want to hear about my days,
the good ones and the bad.
I've got more than your attention, Lord.
I have your love,
and you have mine. Amen.

► **Hallowed be thy name**

I heard once, Lord, that every time a pastor
speaks the benediction,
he's putting your name on all of us.
The words you gave in Numbers 6:24-26, Lord,
are words that put your name on me:
"The Lord bless you and keep you;
the Lord make his face shine upon you
and be gracious to you;
the Lord turn his face toward you
and give you peace."

Three times in that blessing your name is put on me.
Verse 27 reads, "So they will put my name on the
Israelites, and I will bless them."

Lord, I have been labeled.
All of us Christians have been labeled with your name.
We carry your name wherever we go.
It's sort of like wearing a team jersey or a team jacket,
when people look at me and know what school I
    attend.

Lord, when people listen to me
and when people watch what I do,
let them see that I'm one of yours
and that I live to bring your name honor.
I ask the same for everyone on our team, Lord. Amen.

Your kingdom comes, Lord,
whenever your Spirit touches people's hearts
and they believe in you.

Your kingdom comes when water splashes on the
forehead
of a brand-new Christian
brought to you by a missionary.

Your kingdom comes, Lord,
when I speak for you,
when I explain my faith to another person,
when I read the Bible to myself
and I get some real help for my life.

Your kingdom, Lord, is wherever your Word
is preached and taught and celebrated.
I've seen your kingdom in storefront churches in the
city,
in thatched huts on missionary slides,
and right in my own church,
when people cry because they love you so much,
when the pastor tries his best to tell about your love,
and when we all greet each other with your peace.

I live in your kingdom, Lord,
a kingdom that's bigger than time and space,
a kingdom of grace and power, of glory and love,
a kingdom I share with Christians everywhere.
Keep your kingdom coming, Lord, especially through
me.
Amen.

## ► Thy will be done on earth as it is in heaven

I wouldn't be praying to you, Lord,
if I didn't believe that you can make things happen.
You have the power to shape the history of the world
and my history, too.

I want to know your will, Lord.
I want to understand what you want me to do.
All of us Christians—deep down inside—
we want to know what pleases you.
So, Lord, help me to know your will.
Speak to me in the Bible.
Talk to me through people who know you well.
Help me to sort through what's right and wrong.

Then, Lord, when I know your will,
give me the willingness to do it.
It's too easy in my life to do what others want.
I think I spend a lot of time trying to please my
    friends
and others I care about who have opinions of me.
Give me your Spirit
so that I can draw closer to you
to know and to do your will.

I have a feeling, Lord, that even if I didn't pray
"Thy will be done,"
your will would be done anyway.
I'm praying now that your will might be done
especially through me and other Christians. Amen.

# ▶ Give us this day our daily bread

Sometimes, Lord, I forget the basics.
I take a lot of things for granted.
For instance:
the next breath of air I take in,
the food I'll eat at my next meal,
the warmth I'll feel when I climb under the covers in
    bed,
the clothes I'll put on tomorrow morning,
and the money that comes into our home
to provide the things we need just to be alive.

I hardly ever pray for these things, Lord.
I just expect that they'll always be there.
Come to think of it,
a lot of my prayers are about luxuries,
things like 10-speeds and tape decks.
When we Christians pray this part of the Lord's Prayer,
we remember you're not just the God of luxuries and
    extras.
You're the one who gives us what we need to stay
    alive.

There are Christians in the world, Lord,
who pray this prayer with a lot more feeling than I
because they're not sure when they will eat their next
    meal,
whether they'll sleep warm tonight,
or when they'll ever wear clean clothes.
I can't pray this without

thinking of them
and wanting to be a part of your answer to their
prayer. Amen.

► # Forgive us our trespasses as we forgive those who trespass against us

Lord, I find it hard to forgive.
When people hurt me or wrong me
or say bad things about me,
I want to get back at them.
I get angry and stay angry
and remember what they did or said
for a long time.

That's why this part of the Lord's Prayer
is so important for me
and for every Christian who finds it hard to forgive.
Forgiveness doesn't come naturally.
It isn't something we just do without thinking about it.
Forgiveness takes commitment and work.

This prayer teaches us Christians
that the secret of forgiving others
is found in your forgiveness of us.

We're all people who have no right to be forgiven by
     you.
We fail you.
We disappoint you.
Yet "while we were yet sinners, Christ died for us"
     (Romans 5:8).
You forgive us, Lord,
and in your forgiveness
we'll find the example and the power we need
to forgive others, no matter how hard it is. Amen.

► **Lead us not into temptation**

When Jesus was tempted by the devil in the desert,
you were there for him, Lord.
He didn't have to face temptation alone.
You gave him your Word,
and you sent your angels to take care of him.

Lord, I think I've figured out how temptation works.
The devil drops some bait just like in fishing.
It's just the right bait,
something that I like even though it's wrong.
My desire is aroused.
I want what the devil has placed in front of me.
Then I take the bait,
and sin causes lots of problems in my life.

Lord, when the devil goes fishing,
help me to swim away from the devil's bait.
Just as you helped Jesus in his temptations,
help me in mine.
Help me to say with the person who wrote the verse,
"I have hidden your word in my heart
that I might not sin against you" (Psalm 119:11).
Help me, Lord, to know your Word
and to keep it close to my heart
so that the devil will fail when I am tempted. Amen.

Lord, help me to see evil around me.
Open my eyes to what's bad in my life
and in the lives of others.
Sometimes I think I get used to evil,
so used to it that I don't realize how bad it is
and how strong an impact it can have on me.

Lord, help me to see the evil of violence
so that I won't accept violence as a way
of solving problems.
Help me to see the evil of injustice
so that I won't treat others unfairly.
If I don't pay attention to what's evil in life, Lord,
evil may catch me off guard and overpower me.

There are evils in my life, Lord,
that will affect me no matter how aware I may be.
They are parts of life.
There will be sickness,
serious accidents,
and tragedies.
When these difficult times come, Lord,
and when I'm looking death right in the face,
keep me strong,
keep me loyal,
and keep me yours. Amen.

► ## For thine is the kingdom, and the power, and the glory, forever and ever. Amen.

You are in control, Lord.
You control the history of nations,
and you control the history of me.
As I said at the beginning,
you are on top of things, Lord.

Knowing this and believing this
with all other Christians
gives me a great feeling.
I am part of a plan and part of a family
that lasts forever and ever.

There is not much about my life, Lord,
that lasts forever.
Things change
and break
and decay
and grow old.

What I have with you, Lord,
and what I share with Christians of all times and in all
    places
I have forever and ever.
Today I want to say Yes! to your kingdom, your power,
    and your glory.
So, amen, Lord! Forever and ever, amen!

# ► Questions ◄
# about the Future

# ► **What happens after high school?**

I couldn't believe it, Lord.
I met a freshman in high school
who says she already knows what she wants to do
after high school,
after college,
and after graduate school.
She has it all figured out.
I should have asked if she had her retirement plans
nailed down.
I'm glad I didn't.

I hope I have time, Lord, to think about it some
more—
what I'm going to do after high school.
I need to experiment
and to look at all the options.
I'm just not ready to commit for sure to anything.

So, Lord, put in front of me lots of opportunities
to test my strengths
and to find my weaknesses.
Keep me open to new possibilities.
Send people my way who can help me sort through
all the choices I'll need to make
during my last year in high school.
I want to make decisions, Lord,
but not right now. Amen.

# ▶ What kind of car will I drive?

Sometimes, Lord, I think about myself
driving a car as an adult—
my car—
that I've bought for myself.
The only problem I have is that
I never know for sure what kind of car it will be.
Can you help me with this one?

What kind of car-person am I?
Do I look like a 1999 Volvo driver, Lord?
Or would you say I'm a 2001 Corvette type?

How did cars get to be so important, Lord?
I'll admit it—
I think about cars quite often.
Was there ever a time when cars
were seen just as a way of getting from one place to
    another?
I doubt it.
From the start, I bet we human beings
made cars into something much, much more.

I think it would be a good idea, Lord,
if you would remind me and other people my age
that Jesus, the apostle Paul, and George Washington
never drove cars,
and lived quite well without them. Amen.

This really sounds crazy, Lord,
but sometimes I wonder whom I will marry.
I have in my mind this picture of an ideal woman.
She needs to be beautiful, very beautiful,
intelligent,
with a good sense of humor,
able to put up with me and some of my bad habits,
kind,
not too pushy,
and probably not like most of the girls I know right
    now.

That does worry me, Lord,
that I'd have a hard time finding any girl right now
who might qualify for my wife in 10 years or so.
You do have someone in mind, don't you?
All things considered, Lord,
I think marriage was a great idea—
one man and one woman spending their lives together
in faithfulness and love.
I know we human beings haven't been doing our best
at keeping marriage as you want us to keep it,
but I think marriage is still the best idea ever
for how you want a man and a woman to be together.

So . . . can you give me a hint, Lord?
Is it somebody I know now
or somebody I'll meet in the future?
Oh, well, at least you know what I'm looking for.
    Amen.

► **What kind of parent will I be?**

What kind of parent will I be, Lord?
Will I be cranky, moody, and tough?
Or will I be easygoing and happy?
Will I say things like
"Clean up your room!"
or "Where have you been?"
or "You're grounded!"
or "Did you hear me?"
I hope not.

Someone said, Lord,
that people end up being parents
just like their own parents.
Is that what I'll be like, Lord?
Will I be like my parent?
Will I sometimes be too busy to give my child
the gift of time?
Will I sometimes be too quick to criticize
and to correct my child?
Will I use words that are out-of-date
and talk about times my child never heard of?

I suppose I will.
I'll probably make mistakes.
With your help, Lord, I pray that
my child always will know that my love is always
    there,
just as I know that my parent's love is here for me
    today.
Amen.

# ► Will our family always stay close?

Sometimes I wonder, Lord,
if our family always will stay close.
What happens when kids grow up and move out,
and parents get older,
and family members live in different parts of the
country?

Will my parent and I be friends when we're both
adults?
It's hard for me to imagine that.
It does happen, though. I've seen it.

Lord, I do want to be close to my family
after I'm grown up.
I want to hear the same laughter,
and play the same games,
and talk about the same memories,
and be together on holidays
just the way we are now.

I hope it's possible.
Oh, I know, everything can't be the same.
Everybody gets older and maybe a little weaker.
Sometimes grown children have to take care of their
parents.
Now that would be a switch!

I need your help all along the way, Lord,
so that our family is always a family
for as long as we live on earth. Amen.

Lord, I want to be successful.
I don't just mean successful at what I'm doing now—
sports, music lessons, studies, and that kind of thing.
I mean that I want to be successful when I'm older
and on my own.
I want to be able to look at my life and say,
"Hey, not bad. You've done OK."

That's not sinful, is it, Lord?
It's OK to want to be successful, right?

Sometimes I do get confused as to who is successful
and who isn't.
Is success measured by what kind of a car you drive?
Does success depend on what others say about you
at awards banquets?
How important is money if I want to be successful?
And who decides who's successful and who's a flop?
Magazines? TV? Elections?

Right now, Lord, maybe it's best
if I just work at being the best possible me.
Help me to see that the two of us—you and me—
are the most important ones
who determine if I'll be a success or not.
The secret of my success, Lord, is in your hands,
and in mine, too.
I can wait to find out, but I would like you to know—
I'm expecting great things from both of us. Amen.

# ▶ What if I get really sick?

What if I get really sick, Lord?
I don't mean the flu or something that lasts
a couple of weeks.
I mean *really* sick.
What if I get cancer or AIDS?
What if I land in a wheelchair for life?
What if I get sick and can't get better?

I've seen really sick people before.
Sometimes they scare me.
I need to know, Lord, that if I get really sick,
I'll have what it takes to be OK.
What does it take, Lord?
Let's see—faith, hope, prayer, family, friends.
Maybe I'll be OK after all.
It does scare me, though.

I know one thing.
I'll need more than a good doctor if I get really sick.
I'll need you, Lord.
I can count on you, can't I?
A few angels would make me feel better, too.
I know I shouldn't worry about it.
Somehow talking about it with you
makes not worrying about it more possible.
Amen.

# ▶ Will there be a world in 2020 A.D.?

I wonder if there will be a world in 2020 A.D.
I can get real down about this subject, Lord.
Sometimes I think about
a bomb blowing apart the planet with me on it
or a crazy government leader taking control
and turning us all into brainwashed zombies,
or pollution eating away at the ozone layer
and eventually causing the earth to burn up,
or famine not just sweeping Africa but the whole
    world
causing me to be the one with a swollen belly and
    hungry eyes.

Kind of depressing. Right, Lord?
I know these aren't the best kind of thoughts
for me to have,
but I do have them.
I do worry about this world you made, Lord.
I love your world.
I love life.
You must have thought a lot of your world, too.
After all, you came as one of us to live on this planet,
and you died to bring it back to yourself.

When these thoughts and fears about the future come,
    Lord,
help me to keep your planet safe,
so my worst fears are only nightmares
that never come true at all. Amen.

► **What will heaven be like?**

When I die, Lord, and go to heaven,
what will it be like?
I've heard there will be a lot of singing in heaven.
I like to sing, but if you don't mind my saying so,
I hope that there is more to do than just that.

I heard we'll do things in heaven that bring us joy and
    fulfillment.
I like that!
Will there be football in heaven, Lord?
Will there be woodworking?
Will I see my Christian friends?
Will my family get together?

I know.
Most of these questions will have to wait
until I get there.

I have noticed something, Lord.
The things I love the most on earth,
the things that really turn me on
and get my heart pumping,
it seems as if I can never get enough of them.
That points to heaven, doesn't it, Lord?
That means there is a place
where I can have all the joy and fulfillment I want.
Heaven sounds like a great place all right.
I thank you for sending Jesus to die and to rise
and then to prepare a place like heaven for me. Amen.

# ▶ Will hot lunch cooks get to heaven?

Will hot lunch cooks get to heaven, Lord?
I suppose they will,
but on faith alone. Right?
They won't get to heaven
on the merits of their hot lunches!
That's for sure!

Lord, I'll say this as nicely as I can:
I don't like the hot lunches at school.
I wonder sometimes how the cafeteria cooks
can look so happy and be so kind
while they serve food that only a humble teenager
who's too lazy to make his own lunch would eat.

Do they know, Lord?
Do they understand that their food
and my tastes are becoming world-class enemies?
If they don't know, Lord,
would you tell them in a dream or a vision
or something very biblical
so that they come to know the truth?

I like these people, Lord.
You fed 5000.
Help them to do a better job feeding us.
You do have other plans for the feasts of heaven,
don't you, Lord? Amen.